The Blurring of Time

Also by Ronald Moran

Poetry (Books and Chapbooks)

Diagramming the Clear Sky
Fish Out of Water
Getting the Body to Dance Again
Life on the Rim
Greatest Hits, 1965-2000
Saying These Things
Sudden Fictions
So Simply Means the Rain

Criticism

Four Poets and the Emotive Imagination (with George S. Lensing)
Louis Simpson

The Blurring of Time

Ronald Moran

Copyright 2007 by Ronald Moran
ISBN 0-9771263-7-4

Published by Clemson University Press in Clemson, South Carolina.

Copy editing and layout at the press by Wayne K. Chapman (Executive Editor), assisted by Kara McManus.

Cover design by Myers Enlow.

To order copies, visit the Clemson University Press website: www.clemson.edu/press.

Contents

Acknowledgments vii

Part One
Following BB's 2
The Bells of St. Maurice 3
Days Like That 4
Redeeming the Lost 5
The Courtship 6
Tic Tacs 7
The Umbrella 8
After the Game 9
Thanks All Around 10
The Waiting Area of the Dealership 11
Mosquitoes 12
The Sports Bar 13
Origins 14
Finding a Place After Social Security 15
Turning Cold 16
The Offertory 17

Part Two
In Reflective Glass 20
Quintet 21
Some Days 24
October 21, 2005 25
The Man in the Moon 26

Part Three
The Blurring of Time 28
Man with a Metal Detector, Early Morning on the Beach 29
Flight Patterns 30
Recasting the Landscape 31
Discourse of a Mangrove Swamp 32
Dream Merchant 33

Compliance   34
The Natural Order of Things   35
Summer Remedies   36
Borders and Crossings   37
Absence of Light   38
The Weather Forecaster   39
Waking Up to Get the Mail   40
The Prize   41
On a Morning   42

Part Four
The Music of Blackbirds   44
Antecedents of Mercy   45
The Waiting Room of the Cancer Center   46
Allergic Reaction   47
At the Kitchen Table   48
Sounds of a Late Afternoon   49
On My Street   50
Caterpillars   51
The Morning After   52
Waking Up Is a Drug That Disorients   53
Tics   54
On the Exit Ramp   55
Lines for an Elliptical World   56

A Note on the Author   58

Acknowledgments

Some of the poems appeared originally in the following publications: *Abbey* ("At the Kitchen Table," "The Courtship," "Lines for an Elliptical World," "The Waiting Area of the Dealership," "Waking Up Is a Drug That Disorients"), *The Comstock Review* ("The Blurring of Time," "The Man in the Moon"), *Curbside Review* ("Waking Up to Get the Mail"), *Ibbetson Street* ("The Music of Blackbirds"), *Iodine Poetry Review* ("Absence of Light"), *Lilliput Review* ("On a Morning"), *Main Street Rag* ("Borders and Crossings," "On the Exit Ramp," "The Sports Bar," "Tic Tacs"), *Mankato Poetry Review* ("Summer Remedies"), *Northeast* ("Caterpillars"), *Open Cut* ("On My Street"), *Pudding Magazine: The Journal of Applied Poetry* ("Dream Merchant," "Thanks All Around"), *The Same* ("The Prize"), *The South Carolina Review* ("Discourse of a Mangrove Swamp," "Flight Patterns," "Man with a Metal Detector, Early Morning on the Beach," 'My Mother Likes Her Coffee Strong' from "Quintet," "The Offertory," "The Waiting Room of the Cancer Center"), *Tar Wolf Review* ('My Father Is Looking through His Telescope' and 'The Honeymoon' from "Quintet"), *Willard & Maple* ("The Morning After"), and *Yarrow* ("Days Like That").

for Jane

Part One

Following BB's

I followed BB's in perfect arcs
over a meadow, across a creek,
and into a stand of fall colors;
listened on calm days for hits
on brittle leaves. Small birds,
waiting for a flock moving south,
popped out and back in, not my
target or interest. As if married,
copperheads and blacksnakes
cozied up for the long sleep
in the huge rocks my father
hand carried for his back wall,
before which I stood, my air
rifle aimed high, my eyes as
good then as ever—to follow
the first of my irrational flights
to a wood I could never enter.

The Bells of St. Maurice

At six every morning, the bells of St. Maurice rang
on the fringe of the only streets Jews could buy into
in our town, downwind of the hilly homes of rich
Episcopalians, in this town of immigrants, tools,
hardware, ball bearings, steel strapping, where
gentle, red-haired Billy S, a year out of high school,
my age, crossed the strike line at a machine tool plant
and was beaten. Soon the plants moved southeast,
anywhere the help was homegrown like moonshine,
and the churches were Baptist, Methodist, or long-
named like Holiness and Fire Baptized Pentecostal,
and our town shrunk because of why they beat up
Billy, even though the bells tolled right from wrong.

Days Like That

I saw my first stripper
at the Berlin Fair
the day the ophthalmologist
found myopia deep inside

my dilated pupils
and prescribed dark glasses,
which aged me enough
to buy into the tent

where, among men,
I stood at the edge of the stage
on the hard dirt floor
and was chosen.

When she got down to net stockings
and a bejeweled G-string,
she dropped to her knees,
drubbing my red-hot cheeks

with her breasts,
knocking those dark lenses
nearly out of their frame
and me with them.

Whatever they call days like that,
they come rare.

Redeeming the Lost

Trying to impress no one in particular
but everyone in the gym and, mostly,
my hard won sense of self,

I went three for fifty-two in a game,
said George Appleby, older than me,
sitting on our bench with the coach,

like a buddy. Up and down the court,
my right arm quivered, George said, as
if it were warming up for my next shot.

Our coach, red-faced, was feeling his
whiskey, his armor of indifference, its
vapors surrounding him like cologne.

I didn't think to take myself out, only
to make it good, the kind of thinking
on the court or field (or on her porch

the light off, only the two of you left
in the universe) that makes up a mind
to redeem the lost, the irretrievable.

The Courtship

In the middle of the Cold War,
I lived in a bombed-out shelter
of compliance until the all clear

sounded, like the lid of a grate
blown off the top of my head.
On a chance she'd be riding

in a car down the hill that day,
I stepped up, over my debris,
to the light of a diffident sky:

my crossover time, latent blue,
a dressing of cirrus. I took off
my tee shirt, an unlikely act

of courtship if she happened by,
looking over by choice not
chance at me mowing the same

patch of lawn over and over
in front of the clumped cedars,
an offering of my unrehearsed

goods in early summer, time
holding on to its first whisper
of assent, on a burnished day.

TIC TACS

for Jane

Three times this week
you've dropped the Tic Tacs,
wedging them between
your seat and its track,
and each time I tell you
to be more careful,
to put them in a side pocket,
when you remind me
there isn't one in my midget car,
asking me each time,
why do I get so upset
over Tic Tacs
while you adjust your scarf
to the wind, and snap on
the dark glasses we bought
at the ophthalmologist's,
and I'm thinking, as I shift
into reverse, why do I get
so upset over Tic Tacs,
and what am I supposed
to do if I want a Tic Tac,
and what will I do
if your heart closes up
like a sundrop after dark?

The Umbrella

Until I was 33, I owned no umbrella.
What fell fell, and I took it, as when
the showers of Waterville cracked
a morning smile over humped roofs.
The sun ascended like a virgin bride
of the Apocalypse, days like nights.
Sullied, they wore out their welcome.

From November to April, the sun took
a sabbatical in Würzburg, wet snow
slogging the shops of Sanderstrasse,
so I bought a black umbrella. I took
it everywhere, on walks through
familiar woods, to the endless dunes
of deserts, into dreams, as if a charm.

After the Game

On the bench seat in front, my grandson
puts his long arm around his girl, his first,
and talks slowly to her, leaning toward
her small presence. He answers us easily,
too, as if he were an adult. We are coming
back from his game, a victory, competing
for his divided attention with questions:
*Why didn't you blitz on third down? What'd
the coach say? Who's number 30, the fast kid?*
His father drives, and I am sitting in back

with his mother and grandmother. When
we drop his girl home, my grandson walks
her up the stony path to her door, kisses
her, returns to command the front seat.
In a voice and tone I acknowledge, accept,
he says, *Hey Dad, you see me drill that guy
on the kickoff? No, the one I blocked. See me
drop their quarterback twice? I nailed him!*
How long will this take to pass? How long
before he becomes like us, all eyes and ears?

Thanks All Around

Today I am visiting myself in my
study. Cables crawl over the floor
like a festival of snakes, and I am
waiting for a salesman to call me,
to lower the price of the Toyota
I want, even though his manager
showed me, in print, his real cost.
My fault for not being grateful,
more generous and appreciative.
As I left the dealership I thanked
both; they thanked me, wishing
me the best, the salesman telling
me to come by for a visit, to talk.
In my car, waving to them one
last time, I could almost hear
their astonishment at my naivete.

The afternoon crawls, shedding
its skin, light dropping a notch
in the mottled sky. At last I get
up, take a cordless phone, walk
to the end of the driveway, pick
up a packet of mail, opening
first an invitation-like envelope
from the dealership, my hopes
racing, and read an engraved
card that thanks me for buying
a new Toyota, signed by both.
Did I buy it? Is it in the garage
waiting for me to remember it?
Last year a woman called to ask
how I liked the new Dodge truck
I never bought. Or did I buy it?
What do they say to each other
in the buggy garage, that I have
lost my way, that I am holding
them hostage? Whose garage?
What am I hiding from myself?

The Waiting Area of the Dealership

I am sitting in a gun-metal gray chair,
in an alcove, not feeling of this place.
In another chair, a man wipes a tear
off a laptop that is weeping with him.
A woman sitting on the couch talks
on a cell phone as if she were a CEO
in trouble, the regulators closing in.
A string quartet plays Haydn for us
from a ceiling that arcs like a Quonset,
that is beaming down rays of light.
I ask around me, *Are we being saved?*

Mosquitoes

They are swarming in back,
hovering over a drying pool
of mud in a off-zone ditch:
hungry, weak, whining as if
owed a wraparound storm.

I spray myself, to repel their
cargo of virus from laying
me out, like a patch of dead
grass in a yard of high living.
Whose fantasy comes first?

I went to a chic clairvoyant,
to ask, will I be reincarnated
as a better self, a better mass?
That was a mistake. She said,
Get bit. Try to live through it.

The Sports Bar

On a brisk Saturday at the sports bar,
I shoot pool with Harry, my son-in-law,
then sit down at a table near two women
and a guy, to eat and finish our drinks.
The women are already drunk, loud,
having fun, it seems. One asks how
I am. I reply, *Failing the best way I can*,
stock response of a smiling sixty-eight
year old, oldest there by a generation.
The other—a blond, large build, busty—
comes to our table, says she is a stylist,
asks to run her hands through my hair,
the little that's left, cut the shortest of its
failed life, like a soldier's or a sheriff's.
She does, and her breasts nudge me.
When she stops massaging my head,
I say, *That makes my day.* She's happy.
Later, when the three of them finally
untie the knots of their bill, she comes
back, rubs it once, and, as she is leaving,
I call out, *Take care of yourself.* Without
breaking stride, she turns her head,
flashing a tongue stud, and swings
her butt twice. A day on the beach
in July, steamy, surf inviting but big.

Origins

From my study, I am listening
to skateboarders grind down
the street's soft incline. They

sound like a jet, gear and flaps
lowered, sucking in rich air
on a back-up landing pattern

over my house, and I fold my
hands together, as if praying
or pressing a vagrant thought

whose subject is uncertain,
like the origins of suffering
in a corridor behind closed

double doors, at the sterile end
of a waiting room, neither dark
nor light, nor any shade I know.

Finding a Place After Social Security
for Jane

In this building like a dormitory,
I am trying to find us a place to live.
The rooms are either small or huge

like common rooms. Doors open,
close all night, and it is always night.
Someone I know but can't remember

waves and vanishes down the stairs.
All the toilets are stuffed with paper,
and the flusher is the end of a bolt.

I call out, *Where's a clean bathroom?*
I think I am lost. I parked my car
just around a corner I cannot find,

and, standing in absolute dark, I am
becoming used to it, the same dream,
as if we are starting over, at our age.

Turning Cold

In early October my body
turns cold, and I blame
this house, even when
all thermometers read
in the comfort zone. Are
my circuits shorting, bent
T-cells huddling together,

or hormones at last giving
up their territorial holds
to border guards that make
crossing their gates easy
going, in a cagey arithmetic
of age, a cellular rebellion
canceling old animosities?

This changing of seasons
confirms each heartbeat—
the raging of a windstorm,
debris, flakes of errant snow
in the hills, the belly wash
of high water tables, the sun
popping its blood vessels.

The Offertory
for RJC, 1926–2004

At the funeral of an old friend,
I found an offertory check
for two thousand, in a hymnal,
written in the hand of one very

old, and I prayed for guidance
for an uncommitted sin. Was
this a windfall, a gift of grace?
At the reception, I gave it

to the priest, who, knowingly,
shook my shaking hand, as if
to absolve this mortal pause
of mine, this momentary drift

into myself, where the edge
of memory, the rim of a cliff,
dreams of a sharp hang, a cut
of bold lines, falling, falling.

Part Two

In Reflective Glass

The man beside me reflected in glass
walks with a slight limp like mine; mimics
my moves, as if knowing in advance what
I will do, and, of course, he does, as I do.
So I stop finally before a blank storefront
to confront him, to ask, out of playfulness,
why am I his target. It is my father holding
out his hand, as if to take me into his world.
I press my palms to the barrier glass. I form
my words slowly, deliberately, trying to say
to him, *No, I cannot come now, but later, later.*
He has had enough of my excuses, leaves
me touching the warmth of my other palms,
reading the words I form in slow motion.

Quintet

My Father Is Sitting on a Bench

My father is sitting on a bench at the back
of a classroom. His mother has just died,
giving birth to a second brother. His father
will not speak to him and soon he will send
my father away on a whirligig of homes.
He will marry again, my father will come
back home, love his new mother, she will
also die, and he will be sent off again.
My father is upset, sitting alone at the back
of the room, and he will not participate.
I am thinking that is why he will stay back
in kindergarten, but my father the genius
will later skip the second and fourth grades,
and will never talk about himself, that life.

My Mother Is Riding on a Hungarian Float

My mother is riding on a Hungarian float
in Stamford, circa 1924, with another beauty:
two mermaids, wreaths of kelp in their hair.
On the side of the street, a boy, as a whim,
tosses a nail high in the air, no target in mind
but the air it hurries through, and just then,
as my mother looks up, the nail strikes her
right eye, leaving a mark: amber on white.
As a child, I will often ask her to tell me
the story of the nail in her eye. She will say
he did not aim it, just tossed it at will, that
she was a young girl in front of her house
looking up the hill for one of her brothers.
She will say nothing about riding on a float.

The Honeymoon

In Virginia Beach, on his honeymoon,
a riptide took my father swiftly out
to sea, his bride helpless on the shore.
Did she think of such early widowhood
in Stamford, in 1927? In two months
her older brothers would die in the first
sightseeing flight over New York City.
She had the measles then, still a bride
when her thyroid exploded, nine years
to my birth, an only child of two newly-
weds in Virginia Beach: my father, gone
a half mile out when the current gave up,
swimming back, a thin, handsome man,
to his bride, my mother, rooted in sand.

My Father Is Looking through His Telescope

My father is looking through his telescope
and he tells me the names of what he sees.
He wants me to appreciate the heavens
of his understanding. When I look through
the cold eyepiece, I see dots on a black wall.
That is all I will ever see, and my father tries
not to lose his patience, to accept his only
child's confusion of his clear universe.
In the morning, when he lights up his first
cigarette at the table, as my mother stacks
the plates, he is asking himself what will
become of me. As the ash grows longer,
he asks me if I like numbers, and I say,
Yes, Yes, and he flicks the ash in his hand.

My Mother Likes Her Coffee Strong

Your mother likes her coffee strong and her men weak, my father says. Mornings
he makes strong coffee in a two cup pot
that sits on a burner in our kitchen,
the three of us at the table, quiet
but for my father's purring after each
breath, his right index finger resting
on his upper lip, like a mustache.
Why do I keep asking him to stop it?
as if I were the arbiter of sounds
in the most composed time of our day,
before my mother collects evidence:
a tissue in a pocket, a strand of hair,
a faint scent of what-is-it? Not hers.

Some Days

In spring the open windows of All Saints' Episcopal School
admitted the smells of trimmed hedges, lawns, and vines,
inducing a haze in us, like a narcotic, in the third grade,
but I still fought every boy in class, fell for Linda Waters,
and fudged numbers in arithmetic once, feeling so stupid
at what I had missed, my only recourse was to get it right,
at all costs, and what did I know about the costs of nibbling
at arithmetic, of not being able to lose at all, of my fevers?

Early one Saturday, with my mother and father, after
picking mushrooms with pink bellies on the third hole,
on our way home, walking half way up the sloped fairway,
making tracks in the dew, buckets in our hands, I told them,
I wish you were dead, without meaning it or thinking of costs,
and they kept on walking and never said anything.

October 21, 2005

On my father's 104th birthday,
the few of us left in his family sit
around a table. He has not yet
appeared, and I am thinking, What
will he look like, What will he see
through those quiet, blue eyes,
Will he be happy we have come?
This is his first birthday party.
Why don't we light the candles?

The candles on his cake line up
like infantry at an ancient battle,
ready to fire on command, to die
if need be. I want to say to him,
We were both wrong. At this table,
my father tracks me like a tracer.

The Man in the Moon

I could not see the man in the moon
when my father, the engineer, took
me out for walks, saying, *refraction*

reflection, as our shadows stretched
out before us, or trailed after us
like long tails under tall street lights.

I lost the stars, constellations, heroic
names I could only repeat by memory,
while the sky kept revealing to him

its solitary secrets. They touched
him like snowflakes, like droplets,
like the clear voice of the world.

Part Three

The Blurring of Time

It happens anywhere but mostly
in waiting rooms: cancer clinic,
ophthalmologic, orthopedic,

where you look at your watch,
out of sync with the clock
on the wall, if there is a clock,

but probably not, since time,
the issue, is taking a break down
the corridor, behind the door

that the nurse opens, calling
out your name, beckoning you,
saying, *And how are you today?*

and you say, *Fine*, as if no other
reply would make the nurse
happy, as she guides you into

a room where time opens up its
hand, cupping you in its palm,
like a small, imperfect flower.

Man with a Metal Detector, Early Morning on the Beach

What you lost the day before,
this man must crave to enter

his life: to find, touch and hold,
as offshore, combing the sea,

a pelican dove, its beak a blade
piercing the skin of a swell.

I left the balcony to sleep it off.
What? The night before the view,

or the view? It's easy to confuse
anything linear at the beach, all

that flesh hissing in the sun, foam
like wet blessings doing an act

of absolution on swollen feet,
the gritty underside of a life half

in, half out, as if crossing a line
equals the licensing of dreams.

FLIGHT PATTERNS

for Jane

I asked you if living at the end of a runway
bothers you. No answer, but you were asleep,
of course, and slept through the jumbo cargo

jet from Germany—abundant car parts,
maybe cars, too—at three a.m., when most
planes are ferrying drugs from south Florida,

their props breathing hard over the mountain
range north of us, like a lost platoon of tourists
hacking away at the underbrush once the rain

returned with a welcome vengeance.
That's what I thought before I woke up again,
to listen, always listen, to your quick breaths.

Recasting the Landscape

In his kitchen, a farmer turns on
a light before dawn. A DC-9 dips
a wing as if to say, *Hey down there*.
By noon, a field full of furrows
glistens in the Midwest and pants
for breath in the Deep South.
After dusk, the last of the light
becomes the first chimera of roads
that are not roads but channels
into wherever you wanted to go.

Discourse of a Mangrove Swamp

A large exotic bird, all wings, climbs
out of a mangrove swamp, water
moccasins snickering at its clumsy

take-off, small birds ripping the air,
flying their little wings off, trying
to impress. The large bird ponders

tough questions, is exhausted, rests,
all the while thinking of answers.
The swamp drifts off. The moccasin

fights off an urge, lights up a Gauloise
like a critic, swims across the margins
and disappears, taking all the credit.

Dream Merchant

I was invented by your badmen
and I am only one short step
from mining your worst fears.

If you let me, I will be a friend,
confidant, protector. Trust me.
I am much better than others

who peddle a bank of dreams.
If you let them, they will betray
your deepest secret, you know

the one I mean; and the people,
knowing you for the first time,
will avoid you like fruit rotting

in the marketplace, common
grounds to barter one's stock
of virtues, or to trade like this.

COMPLIANCE

I have commerce with the dead and dying
in my dreams, at the height of their living.

They command and I comply easily, as
if their presence completes my emptiness,

my so quick willingness to agree. *Yes, Yes,
I do understand. Which is the way to the crest?*

Over the edge of the roof of a tall building,
I leaned too far without thinking or cause

and listened to death's syntax, its tongues.
Fingers like claws, like talons, I tried to hold

on to the indifferent edge. *I'm not ready yet.*
The dead and dying took up sides over me:

they cheered me on and wept, they offered
advice and consent in a brilliant blue sky.

I could neither hold on nor let the edge
deny me, but they keep at it, *Hold on, Let go.*

The Natural Order of Things

Daydreaming and dementia may be kin,
as in the more you daydream the closer
a relation you become. To let the mind
roam like an errant spotlight, to brighten
momentarily the recesses of a lost minute,

may loosen the trigger finger, that itch
of correspondence in the late night brawl
inside the old singlewide, two deputies
outside, waiting for backup, neighbors
having heard words and a muffled pop.

It's been a good trailer park, no trouble here,
they say, and a daydream that resists
is charged with threat to do bodily harm,
handcuffed, shoved in the caged back seat,
read its rights by a deputy with short hair.

Summer Remedies

To take seriously the rope tricks of cobras
or a hand gripping the top of the world,
to ponder only the most pungent roots—

are only fleeting hedges against adversity.
To climb any further up the grizzled trunk
you must use all your tricks of ascension,

for all the evidence points to our failures
of last summer, when the sun dried us out,
lowering lakes, hurling boaters headfirst

off the bows of runabouts, now marooned
like cars lost in meadows or sitting on top
of cliffs, *For Sale* signs faded by the sun's

resolute mind in an age of white kitchens.
Better to shift scenes than to squander
what remains on the scent of memories.

Hence the newer guests, lowballers by
trade, with loose change to burn, insist
on talking down the moodiness of clerks.

In rooms facing water, the best in the house,
curtains dance to the whims of a breeze,
side to side, like the specters of old lovers.

Borders and Crossings

Where two or three counties rub each other,
politicians avoid the crossings, as in worn out

bridges over angry creeks, no room to turn
a squad car around, no help on the other side,

only flaming tailpipes. You'd think watchdogs
would be the big issue here: green space, spot

zoning. Only crossings matter, nothing else:
defining our lives, on your side, on my side.

Absence of Light

In the far north, absence of light
depresses, long periods of the sun
flattening out, leaving residents

to cope in novel ways with dark,
even in summer when the sun's
arc is like a tired inchworm, barely

rising, a sky of feints, a daylight
that is not light but a limp mimic,
where one's shadow is a singular

monument, the triumph of a day,
and I tally up my blessings, worn
out T-cells stitching a body bag

that claims some few uncommon
days of light left, to patch into
a long, sustained, holding pattern.

The Weather Forecaster

sits on a table in the middle of a room
with one hanging bulb that flickers
like the sun off a nervous lake.

Around the table, the chairs go outside
for a smoke, and the forecaster blinks
off the seconds of an atomic clock.

Outside the landscape bores the moon.
The night is as clear as white wine but
for the smoking chairs, the doubters.

They want more proof, something
like a hole in the sky, a corridor,
a white, white passage of new light.

Waking Up to Get the Mail

One day's mail is like another's,
though waking holds the promise
of mystery, a reason to get out of bed,
dreams still floating like low level clouds

before the concrete sun sears our eyes.
The visitations of our bodies
line up like collectors at the door, hands out-
stretched, their minds on other, happy pursuits.

*

What do I owe them? I keep paying my bills,
all my receipts soaking in my pants pockets.
Last night I stood like a sentinel in a cloud-
burst on a street corner, watching telephone

poles walk out of town, my glasses blurring
like a cataract, smearing like finger paints.
To cars stopping to let me cross the street,
I smiled, waved hello, and said, *Next time.*

The Prize

for Jane

Assigning points and adding them up
provide the proof required to award
the pumpkin of the year, in costume.
If we win, if we are blessed this way,

and if you insist we should escort it
to the ball, we'd better stand in line
at dawn, camping out in our pajamas,
an adventure. That's very important,

but only if the pumpkin cooperates.
As expected, the prize evaporated,
like the flight I dream I can never
board because I cannot find the gate.

I hope you're able to sleep in peace
without aching or a neighbor scaling
the bushy side of our house, an attack
on our unprotected flank, which is what

flanks are for, aren't they? Be careful.
Last night they egged your old car again,
the shame of our street, your legacy, my
luck, our past with plush blue upholstery.

On a Morning

A piece of America simmered in a field
of stalks like a smoldering campfire.
To the north, outside the rim of chaos,
geese flew backwards in inverted Vs,
blackbirds descended into meadows,

into sunken tables of lakes, onto high
tension wires over fairways, waiting
for their beeps and tremors to subside.
Cars and trucks turned on their lights,
and the people were kind to each other.

Part Four

The Music of Blackbirds

On high-tension lines on Woodruff,
off the Interstate, blackbirds look
like notations on a musical staff,

as if they felt songs in the lines
and were scoring them for us,
to be read and known at this place

most of us dread passing through:
cars, trucks panting for the longest
stoplight in town to turn. One bird

flew off, changing a measure, then
another, and the tone took a leap:
new music in a commerce of beats,

as the sound inside a gray Pontiac
next to me throbbed like a migraine,
its driver in pursuit of going deaf

before he's 25; and, as uncharitable
as this must seem, it didn't matter
the day when the birds wrote music.

Antecedents of Mercy

Like knock-kneed calipers of haste, birds
of dissimilar feathers flap out of breath,
out of air above a barren scape, one cast
of too bent timber and misshapen brick.

Here it is that birdsongs make soft pitches.
Now one, then another murmur like prayer,
like vespers, like the confessions of saints.
Behind the veil of intimacy, they submit.

The birds quiver like bats. At crossroads,
the homeless hold the same scruffy signs.
On freight trains, boxcars open their doors.
Inside, straw gathers in corners, mercifully.

The Waiting Room of the Cancer Center

Hanging from the high, arched ceilings
of the cancer center, light fixtures look
like spaceships. Wooden beams brace
the ceiling above a huge waiting room.

Whoever we are, why ever we're here,
we all look as if we're waiting for our
flights to be called. Voices like blunt
echoes bounce off the ceiling, the walls.

The public address system announces
a flight to be boarded: two passengers
rise, walk, one with help, to the gate.
Palm trees pair off like lovers strolling.

I know I have joined a killing society,
all of us assassins or targets, whatever
the moment declares: to aim the rifle
or to stand up straight against the wall.

Allergic Reaction

Almost dark in December and Jane
is napping off her pain, my time
to read a poem on *Lucia* at the Met,
and sniffle, sneeze, nearly tear up,

not at the poem, which is funny, or
the opera, which is not, but at what-
ever coexists with the warm air
that tunnels through my ductwork.

Every year the *Ducts R Me* man
places in my mailbox his grisly ad
of the life that inhabits our ducts,
and I think of the bodily debris

a Kirby Vacuum Cleaner man once
deposited on our living room rug,
in his free demonstration just after
Jane took ill, and now I am too far

removed from the arts to reconnect.
What I need is a new box of Kleenex,
clear passage through my mine field
of minutia, and Jane to awake happy.

At the Kitchen Table
for Jane

I'm holding onto the edge of the table
while you line up your pills
and six almonds, and I'm thinking
of how it was for you before
your body gave in to its legacy.

If I were you, I would ask me,
Why are you holding onto the table?
as if the seas are fifteen feet, the others
at our sitting back in their cabins,
having forgotten to take their pills.

Which is what I'm focusing on now—
the pills of our history, as we sit here,
one window blind breaking the sun
into chunks of light, as even as time,
like bands of gold on the table.

Sounds of a Late Afternoon

Jane's been sleeping for an hour,
and I think I hear running water
over the whoosh of air in my den:
her cells replenished, refreshed,

whatever happens after the very
sick, having weakened in the late
afternoon, fall asleep and awaken.
I think I hear her steps in the hall,

coming to where I am pretending
to read but thinking, Is that you?
I was reading a smart and funny
poem by David Kirby. Earlier,

I read of two Americans having
won the Nobel Prize in medicine
for learning how the sense of smell
works, as in knowing perfumes

or fine wines, not the cheap stuff
I drink after Jane's nap, as we sit
in the parlor and wait for a timer
to tick our supper down: she's

feeling the best of all day and I'm
drinking a tart, fruity chardonnay.
I ask, *How's the coffee?* She says,
Fine, her face bright, eyes perky:

sleep, the health machine, having
its set of overriding commands.
But she's still asleep, so I'll wake
her once I finish reading the poem

I drifted away from, in one of his
thirty, maybe forty line sentences,
brought that far by a movement
like familiarity, lifeline to a past.

On My Street

A man is riding home from work
on his Honda motorcycle,
leaning forward like the bike.

Together, they are a question mark
parting dusky air, a sunset union,
an integer in the long waning.

Caterpillars

The caterpillars that start up by mid-morning
in this hot August are taking a siesta after lunch.
As I walk down my driveway to check the mail,
my neighbor, dressed in shorts and a tee shirt,
is wearing stomping boots.

He wipes off the bottoms of his boots, takes
back inside a can of insecticide and the rough
broom he uses to sweep the bodies onto
his lawn or into cement cracks. Those scaling
his brick veneer or navigating angles, he gasses.

Often, when I finish a stunning book of poems
or one poet's terrific work featured in a magazine,
I cannot write a line of poetry afterwards, though
I want to, thinking, *This is what you have done
for me. Thanks. Here's what I can do for myself.*

My words hump across the page,
open targets on a white driveway, and the guy
down the street, refreshed from iced tea and a nap,
insecticide in hand, stands his broom at parade rest,
and, checking out his boots, stomps once, then twice.

The Morning After
November 3, 2004

On her morning walk, a neighbor
who calls the sheriff every time
a child crosses her lawn asked me,
as I stooped to pick up my paper,

Are you a Bush man? I answered,
No, I prefer the comfort of walled-
in spaces, a thermostat, and clothes.
She kept walking at a good clip.

I should have called out to her,
Hey, I'm only kidding, but I think
I might have meant it, or some
of it, at least the part about walls,

and now I'm thinking the sheriff
may want to come by, something
about harassment, about a man
roaming the bush country, naked.

Waking Up Is a Drug That Disorients

I sleep in intervals, like drips in an IV,
and another poem forgets to remember.

Some need to meditate, as on the bones
of spiders on dingy sills in dark rooms.

That lost part of me waits like a cocoon—
skittish spirit, niche dweller on the moon.

Tics

One takes his head
in both hands, twists
it like an adjustment.

Another touches her
fingers to her mouth,
slapping both sides

of her head so quick
only a sound exists,
while the two-finger

tapper is still waiting
for the border guard
of pathways to do it

again, that body jerk
from so far inside
only circuits know,

and what they know
is like ancient law,
like carvings of time.

On the Exit Ramp

A homeless man stands on a triangle
at the I-85 exit ramp, holding a sign,
"Will Work For Food." Drivers lock
into a long stop light. It is raining,
his hair sticks to his neck, shoulders,
his blue shirt darkening in the late
afternoon, as if mirroring his mood.
His arms tire from holding the sign.
He is young to give in to the street,
and I wonder if a simpler time
might suit him better, if ever
there were one, and I remember
my first trip South with my parents,
driving through Georgia on Route 17,
a chain gang working the shoulder
of hard red clay, and I dropped
a pack of my cigarettes to them,
and one grinned, my age, his teeth
still white. From our rear window,
I watched him check out the guard
before he leaned over to pick it up.

Lines for an Elliptical World

To see steam rising
in the middle of a field
without furrows,

one must listen
to the grammar of the brain,
to a spiral of thought
unraveling

like the web of the world
spun out of lines
into a flawless text.

A Note on the Poet

A Note on the Poet

Ronald Moran was born in Philadelphia and moved to New Britain, Connecticut, when he was 10. He received his BA from Colby College and his MA and PhD from Louisiana State University. After having taught at the University of North Carolina for nine years, he joined the Clemson University faculty in 1975, and retired twice, first in 1998 and then in 2000. He served in a number of positions at Clemson, including Professor and Head of the Department of English, Associate Dean, and Interim Dean. In 1969-70, he was Fulbright Lecturer at the University of Würzburg in Germany. He has published nine books/chapbooks of poetry, including *Saying These Things*, the inaugural volume of poetry issued by the Clemson University Digital Press in 2004. His work also includes a trilogy of chapbooks—*Sudden Fictions* (Juniper Press, 1994), *Getting the Body to Dance Again* (Pudding House, 1995, winner of the National Looking Glass Poetry Chapbook Competition), and *Diagramming the Clear Sky* (Pudding House, 2006)—each narrated by his character "Jonathan" about Jonathan's family and the citizenry in a mill town in the Carolinas. In addition, Moran is the author of one book of literary criticism and co-author of another. His poems and essays are widely published in magazines such as *Abbey, Commonweal, Comstock Review, Main Street Rag, North American Review, Northeast, Northwest Review, Pudding Magazine, South Carolina Review, Southern Review*, and *Yankee*. Moran and his wife, Jane, live in Simpsonville, South Carolina.

www.ingramcontent.com/pod-product-compliance
Lightning Source LLC
Chambersburg PA
CBHW031127160426
43192CB00008B/1137